Through the Eyes of CHILDREN

ISRAEL

Connie Bickman

Published by Abdo & Daughters, 4940 Viking Drive, Suite 622, Edina, Minnesota 55435.

Library bound edition distributed by Rockbottom Books, Pentagon Tower, P.O. Box 36036, Minneapolis, Minnesota 55435.

Printed in the United States.

Cover Photo credit: Connie Bickman
Interior Photo credits: Connie Bickman

Edited by Julie Berg

Library of Congress Cataloging-in-Publication Data

Bickman, Connie.
   Israel / Connie Bickman
     p. cm. -- (Through the Eyes of Children)
   ISBN 1-56239-330-8
   1. Israel-- Description and travel--Juvenile literature.
   [1. Israel-- Description and travel.] I. Title. II. Series.
   DS107.6.B53   1994   94-29483
   956.94--dc20   CIP
                                   AC

Contents

Introduction to Israel

Israel is an unusual country.
It is very old and very young at the same time.
The nation of Israel is over 3,000 years old.
But Israel has only been an independent state since 1948.

In ancient times, the Land of Israel was the home of many Jews.
Then Romans took over the land and sent most of the Jews away.
For hundreds of years they were scattered all over the world.
Finally, they began to return to the Land of Israel.
They built new houses and farms and cities.
Now the old Land of Israel is the new State of Israel.

The Bible calls Israel "the Promised Land of the Hebrew Nation."
This was the land where Jesus was born.
The first people were known as Hebrews or the Children of Israel.
Today they are called Jews, after the biblical kingdom of Judah.

Today, five million people live in the small country of
Israel.
These people come from all around the world.
This is called immigrating or aliyah.
Many came from Russia and Ethiopia.
Most of the population are Jews.
Other people include Muslims (Arabs), Christians, Druze
and Bedouin.
The money used in Israel is called the shekel.

The official languages of Israel are Hebrew and Arabic.
On the streets you will hear many languages;
Russian, English, Hungarian, French, Persian, Spanish,
and Yiddish.
This is because immigrants to Israel come from more
than 80 countries.
One word you may hear often is Shalom (pronounced
sha-LOME).
Shalom means hello and it means goodbye.
Shalom also means peace.

Israel is at the crossroads of three continents:
Asia, Europe, and Africa.
Israel's neighbors are Lebanon, Syria, Jordan and Egypt.
The Mediterranean Sea, the Great Syrian-African Rift,
and the Red Sea all touch Israel's shores.
Israel has sandy beaches, rolling hills, ripe farmland, and
ragged deserts.
You can ski in the mountains or swim in the sea.
Israel has historic buildings, old temples and tall
skyscrapers.
Israel is a country of old and new, living side-by-side.

ISRAEL

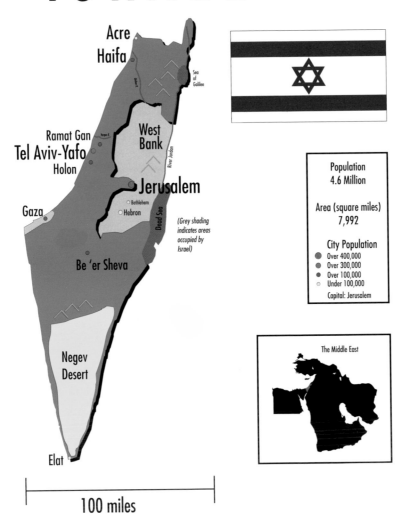

ISRAEL

Acre
Haifa

Sea
of
Galilee

Ramat Gan

West
Bank

Tel Aviv-Yafo

River Jordan

Holon

Jerusalem

○ Bethlehem

Gaza

○ Hebron

Dead Sea

(Grey shading
indicates areas
occupied by
Israel)

Be 'er Sheva

Negev
Desert

Elat

100 miles

Population
4.6 Million

Area (square miles)
7,992

City Population
● Over 400,000
● Over 300,000
● Over 100,000
○ Under 100,000

Capital: Jerusalem

The Middle East

Meet the Children

These children are taking a walk through old Jerusalem.
Jerusalem is the capital of the State of Israel.
Its name means "City of Peace."

This little boy is wearing his favorite hat.
He lives in the city of Tel Aviv.
Today he is visiting Jerusalem on a holiday.

What's Good to Eat?

Kosher (KOE-sher) means to follow the laws of the Jewish religion.

This includes laws about eating food.

These laws say there are three kinds of foods–dairy, meat and pareve.

Dairy foods are milk, butter, cheese, and products made from milk.

Meat includes poultry, lamb, beef and food that have meat in them.

Pareve foods are fruit, vegetables, nuts, fish, and grains (like breads and crackers).

Jews have to follow the laws and eat kosher.

This means dairy and meat food may not be eaten or cooked together.

Pareve foods can be eaten with meat or dairy foods.

Pork and shellfish are not eaten.

They are not kosher.

This man is selling pita bread.
Pita is a flat bread that opens like an envelope.
Some people fill it with felafel (fa-LAY-fil).
This is deep-fried mashed chick peas (garbonzo beans).
A sauce called tehina (TA-hee-nee) is poured on top.
It is made from sesame seeds.
Many kinds of foods can be added to a pita sandwich.
Other favorite foods are humus, kebab, baklava, and pizza!

People shop in open-air markets.
They buy fresh vegetables and fruit for dinner.
Israel is one of the world's leaders in agriculture.
Farmers use solar energy and drip irrigation to help their crops.
They say they grow the world's largest strawberries!

These children like cotton candy.
They are at a celebration in the old city of Jerusalem.

What Do They Wear?

These skullcaps are worn by many Jewish men and boys.
It is part of their religion.
Women and girls wear scarves or hats when they go to the synagogue (SIN-ah-gog) which is where Jewish people go to pray.

This boy is wearing the traditional dress of a Hasidic (hah-SID-ic) Jew. His hair is long and in a braid under his hat.
He is from a community of Orthodox Jews led by a rabbi (RA-by), who is considered a holy person.
Do you see the T-shirts in the store he is passing? They are for sale to the tourists in Jerusalem.

These girls are wearing uniforms.
They are on their way to school.
They are walking on the stone streets of Jerusalem.

Where Do They Live?

These children live in the old city of Jerusalem.
All buildings in Jerusalem's old and new cities
have to be made of a sandy-gold Jerusalem
stone.
It is a law that was made in 1918.
Old Jerusalem has a population of 27,000.
There are separate parts of the city for Jews,
Christians, Armenians, and Muslims.
Each section has their own religions and beliefs.

Large cities have houses and apartments for
families to live in.
In the countryside many homes are made of
cement and stone.

Some families live in kibbutzim (KEY-buts-em).
A kibbutz is a type of farm where many families
live together.
They share in the work and profits.
They have their own schools and grow most of
their own food.
There are more than 200 kibbutzim in Israel.

These children live at Kibbutz Shluchot.
They have 380 cows on their dairy farm.
They have 80,000 chickens.
They grow vegetables in a greenhouse.
They also have a fish hatchery.
One hundred fifty families live at Kibbutz
Shluchot.
They help each other take care of the farm.

Getting Around

Israel has modern transportation.
There are cars, buses, trains, and taxi cabs.
There are also ships, boats, and airplanes.
The airport is named Ben Gurion International Airport.
Israel has one subway train.
It runs from Central Mount Carmel to downtown Haifa.
The trip only takes nine minutes!

Other ways to travel are by bicycle or donkey.
These boats are in the marina in Tel Aviv.
They are used for fishing.

School is Fun!

These two Jewish boys are playing at school.
They go to the Jerusalem Great Synagogue.
They wear skullcaps on their heads.
They dress in slacks, shorts and shirts like you do.

Most Arab children go to Arabic-language schools.
They learn about Arab history and culture.

When Israeli boys and girls turn 18 they go into the army. The army is called the Israel Defense Force.
Men are in the army for three years.
Women are in the army for two years.
After the army they go to college.

These girls are dressed in the uniforms of their school.
They have backpacks with homework just like you do!

This school girl is at the
Eighth Station of the
Cross in Jerusalem.
She is reaching for holy
water to bless herself.
The words at the station
are written in Latin.
They are on the wall of a
Greek monastery.
There are 14 Stations of
the Cross in Jerusalem.

How Do They Work?

This young boy is selling posters.
The picture in the poster is of the Dome of the Rock.
It is a very special place where Muslims go to pray.
The wall in front is the Western Wall.
That is a special place for the Jewish people.

This boy is selling food.
He is balancing a tray of bread on his head.
He is working by the Church of the Holy Sepulchre.
That is a church were Christians worship.
It is built over the tomb of Jesus.

Their Land

Israel is a very historic land.
The oldest known city in the word, Jericho, is in Israel.
The Sea of Galilee is the world's lowest freshwater lake.
The Jordan River is the world's lowest river bed.
The Dead Sea is the world's lowest point above water.
(Did you know there are no fish in the Dead Sea?)

Israel has many important archaeological sites.
This one is Bet She'an.
It is one of the oldest cities in the Near East.
The city was destroyed by an earthquake many years ago.
Archaeologists are working to rebuild the city.

Bethlehem, Nazareth and Jerusalem are in Israel.
This picture of the Western Wall is in Jerusalem.
It is also called the Wailing Wall.
The gold temple in the background is the Dome of the
Rock.

Life in the City

You will see people praying everywhere in Jerusalem.
This little girl is reading from a Hebrew prayer book.
Hebrew is much different than English.
It doesn't have any vowels!
This book is called a Siddur (SY-der).
Does it look like it is upside down to you?
That is because Hebrew is read from right to left.

Life in Jerusalem is always interesting.
You will see Arabs dressed in long flowing gowns.
Next to them you may see a little boy wearing a T-shirt and jeans.
It is a mix of new and old ways of life.

Tel Aviv is a very modern city.
It is Israel's largest city.
There are theaters, zoos, fancy hotels and lots of sandy beaches.
The name Tel Aviv means "Hill of Spring."
Tel Aviv is part of another city named Jaffa.
Jaffa is one of the oldest cities in the world.
Its name means "beautiful."

This boy is standing on the road overlooking Bethlehem. Bethlehem is where Jesus was born.
It is on a hilltop surrounded by rocky pastures.

Family Living

This family is ready to go to the beach.
They are a modern family from the city.

These twin boys are
resting with their
mother.
They have been
shopping in the city
and are tired!

Do you see the gold
crown this girl is
wearing?
She was with her
mother at a birthday
party.
Children in Israel like
to have parties just like
you do.

What are Traditions?

These Israelis are dressed in traditional clothing for their dance.

They are celebrating the Festival of Shavuot.

It is a spring holiday.

It celebrates the giving of the Torah to the Jewish people.

The Torah is the first five books of the Jewish Bible.

It is Israel's national book.

Children are lined up with baskets of fruit as an offering. They are part of a traditional gathering. They are celebrating the Festival of Shavuot with dances and plays.

The square in old Jerusalem is filled with people.
They are celebrating Israel's independence.
They are gathered on Jerusalem Day, a traditional holiday. People everywhere are waving the Israeli flag.

This Jewish boy is putting paper in a stone crack of the Western Wall.
It is a prayer.
It is a tradition.
Another tradition for the Jews is Shabbat (sha-BOT).
Shabbat means "seventh day."
All the stores are closed from sundown Friday to sundown Saturday.
The buses stop and the streets are empty.
Shabbat is a weekly holiday.

Another celebration is called Simhat (SIM-ot) Torah.
The Torah scrolls are carried around the synagogue.
People are happy and singing.
Then scrolls are opened and read again from the beginning.
It takes a year to finish reading the Torah scrolls.
Simhat Torah is a yearly tradition.

Just For Fun!

Fishing is always fun!
These boys are hoping to catch a big one today.
They are fishing in a bay that goes into the
Mediterranean Sea.

Children are the Same Everywhere

It is fun to see how children in other countries live. Many children have similar ways of doing things. Did you see things that were the same as in your life? They may play and go to school and have families just like you. They may work, travel and dress different than you.

One thing is always the same: that is a smile. If you smile at other children, they will smile back. That is how you make new friends. It's fun to have new friends all over the world!

Glossary

Aliyah - Hebrew word for immigrating or "going up."

Arabic - The language spoken by Arab or Muslim people.

Archaeology - Study of sites, buildings and belongings left by ancient people.

Bedouin - Arab herdsman, traditionally dressed in flowing robes, riding camels across the deserts and pitching tents for a campsite.

Druze - Villagers who live mainly in the mountain ranges of Galilee and in the Golan Heights area.

Felafel - Deep-fried balls of mashed chick peas (garbanzo beans).

Hasidic - Orthodox Judaism led by a rabbi, following strict rules of the Torah.

Hebrew - Early name for the Jewish people. Also the language spoken in the days of the Bible.

Kibbutz - A type of farm or commune where all the people share in the work and property.

Kosher - A Hebrew word meaning right, proper, following the law of the Jewish religion.

Muslim - People who believe in Islam, a religion founded in Arabia.

Rabbi - A religious teacher.

Shabbot - A day of rest. Everyone rests from sundown on Friday until it is dark on Saturday.

Shalom - A Hebrew word meaning hello, goodbye, and peace.

Shavuot - The word means "weeks" in Hebrew. In Europe little children begin to study Torah on Shavout. That is the time the Torah was first given to the Jewish people.

Siddur - Jewish prayer book.

Synagogue - A Greek word that means "assembly." It is the name of a Jewish temple.

Torah - The first five books of the Jewish Bible.

Yiddish - Language spoken by European Jews. It is a combination of German, Hebrew and other languages.

Index

About the Author/Photographer

Connie Bickman is a photojournalist whose photography has won regional and international awards.

She is retired from a ten-year newspaper career and currently owns her own portrait studio and art gallery. She is an active freelance photographer and writer whose passion it is to travel the far corners of the world in search of adventure and the opportunity to photograph native cultures.

She is a member of the National Press Association and the Minnesota Newspaper Photographers Association.

DATE DUE